TOUCHSTONE

WORKBOOK 1B

MICHAEL MCCARTHY

JEANNE MCCARTEN

HELEN SANDIFORD

CAMBRIDGE
UNIVERSITY PRESS

CAMBRIDGE
UNIVERSITY PRESS

University Printing House, Cambridge CB2 8BS, United Kingdom

One Liberty Plaza, 20th Floor, New York, NY 10006, USA

477 Williamstown Road, Port Melbourne, VIC 3207, Australia

314–321, 3rd Floor, Plot 3, Splendor Forum, Jasola District Centre, New Delhi – 110025, India

103 Penang Road, #05-06/07, Visioncrest Commercial, Singapore 238467

Cambridge University Press is part of the University of Cambridge.

It furthers the University's mission by disseminating knowledge in the pursuit of
education, learning and research at the highest international levels of excellence.

www.cambridge.org
Information on this title: www.cambridge.org/9781107691254

First published 2005
Second Edition 2014

20 19 18 17 16 15 14 13 12 11 10 9 8

Printed in Great Britain by CPI Group (UK) Ltd, Croydon CR0 4YY

A catalog record for this publication is available from the British Library.

ISBN 978-1-107-67987-0 Student's Book
ISBN 978-1-107-62792-5 Student's Book A
ISBN 978-1-107-65345-0 Student's Book B
ISBN 978-1-107-63933-1 Workbook
ISBN 978-1-107-67071-6 Workbook A
ISBN 978-1-107-69125-4 Workbook B
ISBN 978-1-107-68330-3 Full Contact
ISBN 978-1-107-66769-3 Full Contact A
ISBN 978-1-107-61366-9 Full Contact B
ISBN 978-1-107-64223-2 Teacher's Edition with Assessment Audio CD/CD-ROM
ISBN 978-1-107-61414-7 Class Audio CDs (4)

Additional resources for this publication at www.cambridge.org/touchstone2

Contents

Out and about

Lesson A — Away for the weekend

 1 **What's the weather like?**

Vocabulary **A** Write two sentences about each picture.

1. *It's hot.*
   It's sunny.

2. _____

3. _____

4. _____

5. _____

6. _____

B Answer the questions. Write true answers.

1. How many seasons do you have in your city? What are they? _____

2. What's your favorite season? Why? _____

3. What kind of weather do you like? Cold weather? Hot weather? _____

4. What's the weather like today? Is it warm? _____

5. What's the weather usually like at this time of year? _____

6. Does it ever snow in your city? If yes, when? _____

2 I'm waiting for a friend.

Grammar | **Complete the conversation. Use the present continuous.**

Erin Hi, Ken. It's Erin. Where are you?

Ken Oh, hi, Erin. I'm at the beach. I _'m spending_ (spend)
the day with Tom. It's beautiful here today! It's, uh . . .

Erin Nice. . . . I'm so happy you _____ (have) fun.

Ken Yeah. We _____ (relax).
We _____ (not do) anything
special – I mean, I _____ (read)
a book, and Tom _____ (swim).
How about you? Are you at work?

Erin No. I _____ (not work) today.

Ken Oh, right. So, where – oops! Uh, I'm sorry.
I _____ (eat) ice cream. I'm starving.

Erin Yeah, me too. I _____ (eat) a cookie.

Ken Really? So, where are you? I mean, are you at home?

Erin No, I'm at Pierre's Café. I _____ (wait)
for a friend. He's very late.

Ken Oh, really? Who?

Erin You!

3 About you

Grammar and vocabulary | **Are these sentences true or false for you right now? Write _T_ (true) or _F_ (false).
Then correct the false sentences.**

1. __F__ I'm eating dinner right now.
   I'm not eating dinner right now. I'm doing my homework.

2. ____ I'm using a computer.
   _____

3. ____ My family is watching TV.
   _____

4. ____ My friends are working.
   _____

5. ____ It's snowing.
   _____

6. ____ My best friend is skiing.
   _____

1 All about sports

Vocabulary | **A** Write the names of the sports or kinds of exercise under the pictures.

1. _____volleyball_____

2. _____

3. _____

4. _____

5. _____

6. _____

7. _____

8. _____

9. _____

B Complete the chart with the words in part A.

People play . . .	People do . . .	People go . . .
volleyball		

C Answer the questions. Write true answers.

1. What sports do you play? How often? _I play volleyball on Wednesdays and_
   basketball on the weekends.

2. What sports do your friends play? _____
   _____

3. Do you ever go biking? _____
   _____

4. What sports do people in your country like? _____
   _____

2 What are you doing?

Grammar | **Complete the conversations with present continuous questions.**

1. Joe   Hey, Luis! _What are you doing_ (What / you / do) ?
   Are you at home?

   Luis   No, I'm at the park. I'm playing tennis.

   Joe   Really? _____ (you / play)
   with Janet?

   Luis   No, I'm playing with John today.

   Joe   Oh. So, _____ (you / have / fun) ?

   Luis   No, I'm not. You know, it's raining here, and it's cold.

   Joe   That's too bad. _____ (you / play)
   right now? In the rain?

   Luis   Yes, we are. And it's my turn to serve. Hold on a minute. . . .

   Joe   So, um, _____ (you / win) ?

   Luis   Uh, no. I'm not playing very well today.

   Joe   Is it because you're talking on your
   cell phone?

2. Janet   Hi, Kelly. _____ (How / you / do) ?

   Kelly   Hi. Great. How are you? _____ (you / work)
   this summer?

   Janet   Yes, I'm working at a gym. I'm teaching there. It's fun.

   Kelly   Really? _____ (What / you / teach) ?

   Janet   Aerobics.

   Kelly   Cool. So, _____ (you / do) other things?
   I mean, _____ (you / swim), too?

   Janet   Yeah. There's a pool at the gym. So, _____
   (you / do) anything special this summer?

   Kelly   Well, no. I'm living in my sister's apartment. She's in
   San Francisco this summer.

   Janet   Really? _____ (What / she / do)
   there?

   Kelly   She's working in a restaurant.

   Janet   _____ (she / meet) a lot of
   new people?

   Kelly   Oh, yes. She's having a good time.

1 Keep the conversation going!

Conversation strategies | Complete the conversation with the follow-up questions in the box.

Where are you working?	✓ What are you doing?
Are you practicing your languages?	So, why are you studying Spanish and Portuguese?
What classes are you taking?	Are you enjoying your classes?

Alex Hey, Kate. How's it going?

Kate Good. How are things with you?

Alex Great. But I'm really busy this summer.

Kate Really? *What are you doing?* _____

Alex Well, I'm taking a couple of classes, and I'm working.

Kate Wow! You're working and studying? _____

Alex I'm taking Spanish and Portuguese.

Kate That's interesting. _____

Alex Yeah, I really am. I'm learning a lot!

Kate That's great. _____

Alex Well, I'm thinking about a trip to South America.

Kate That's exciting!

Alex Yeah, and that's why I'm working two jobs, you know.

Kate Right. _____

Alex Well, I'm working at a Peruvian restaurant from 11:00 to 5:00, and I'm working at a Brazilian music club at night.

Kate Really? Wow! _____

Alex Yes, I am! I'm speaking Spanish all day and Portuguese all night.

Kate That's really cool! But when do you sleep?

Alex That's a problem. Sometimes I sleep in class.

Kate Oh, right. That *is* a problem.

2 Asking follow-up questions

Conversation strategies **Complete two follow-up questions for each comment.**

1. "I don't play sports, but I often go running with a friend."

   Really? Where _do you go running_ ?
   How often _____ ?

2. "My parents are on vacation this month."

   That's nice. Where _____ ?
   Are they _____ ?

3. "My grandparents are visiting this week."

   Really? Where _____ ?
   How often _____ ?

4. "I'm working nights this summer."

   Really? Where _____ ?
   What time _____ ?

3 Oh, that's good.

Conversation strategies **Read these people's comments about their summer activities. Complete the responses. Then ask follow-up questions.**

1. I'm really enjoying my vacation this summer.

   Oh, that's _good_ .
   What are you doing ?

2. I'm not doing anything exciting. I'm just reading a lot.

   That's _____ .
   _____ ?

3. I'm not enjoying this summer at all. I'm working ten hours a day.

   Really? That's _____ .
   _____ ?

4. I'm just relaxing, and I'm watching a lot of TV.

   Hey, that's _____ .
   _____ ?

5. I'm exercising a lot at the gym this summer.

   That's _____ .
   _____ ?

6. What vacation? I'm painting my house right now.

   Really? That's _____ .
   _____ ?

1 An advice column

Reading | **A Which sports and exercises do you do? Check (✓) the boxes.**

☐ aerobics   ☐ biking   ☐ skiing   ☐ volleyball
☐ basketball   ☐ running   ☐ soccer   ☐ weight training

B Read the advice column. Match the problems with the Sports Professional's advice.

FITNESS TALK

Do you have a question about exercise? Write to Steven, the Sports Professional, for help and good advice.

1. John: I never exercise. I drive to work, and I sit all day. I hate sports, and I don't like the gym. I know it's a good idea to exercise, but how do I start?

_____

2. Amy: I'm really busy this year. I'm going to school, and I'm working part-time at night. I like exercise, but I don't have a lot of time. Help! _____

3. Bill: I do weight training at the gym every day. I usually love exercise, but these days, it's boring. I think I need a break. What do you think?

a. The Sports Professional: Slowly add exercise to your weekly routine. Walk or ride a bike to work – don't drive. Use the stairs, not the elevator. Clean the house, or do the laundry. Just do something – and start today!

b. The Sports Professional: You're right. You need a break. Try exergaming for a change. There are a lot of different types of activities, and each one helps your body in a different way. Don't stop your weight training, and remember, running is always good for you, too.

c. The Sports Professional: Yes, I know the problem, but try and make time. Experts say we need 30 minutes of exercise five times a week. So, do aerobics for 15 minutes in the morning. Go to school. Then go running for 15 minutes in the evening after work.

C Read the advice column again. Then answer the questions.

1. Is John getting enough exercise these days? _____

2. Does John like sports? _____

3. Amy is busy this year. What is she doing? _____

4. What is Amy's problem? _____

5. How often does Bill go to the gym? _____

6. What does Bill do at the gym? _____

2 Write your own advice.

Writing **A** Look again at the advice column on page 56. Find two imperatives the Sports Professional uses in each piece of advice.

Try exergaming for a change.

B Make imperatives for advice. Match the verbs with the words and expressions.

(Don't)	be	aerobics in the morning	*Don't be shy.*
	buy	at least five times a week	*Buy some good running shoes.*
	do	shy	
	drive	some good running shoes	
	exercise	to work	
	watch	TV all the time	

C Read the problems. Reply to each person. Give two pieces of advice using imperatives. Use the ideas above or your own ideas.

1. **Joe:** I watch sports on TV all the time. I'm watching the Olympics this month. It's great, but I don't do any sports. What sports are fun?
   The Sports Professional: *Try a lot of different sports. I like volleyball, tennis, and swimming. Also,* _____

2. **Anita:** This fall, we're playing soccer at school. I'm not enjoying it very much, especially when it's cold! Also, I'm not very good. Help!
   The Sports Professional: _____
   _____

3. **David:** I like exercise, but I'm lazy! I usually exercise for two or three weeks, but then I need a break. Do you have any advice?
   The Sports Professional: _____
   _____

Unit 7 Progress chart

What can you do? Mark the boxes. ☑ = I can . . . ? = I need to review how to . . .		To review, go back to these pages in the Student's Book.
Grammar	☐ make present continuous statements.	66 and 67
	☐ ask present continuous questions.	68 and 69
Vocabulary	☐ name at least 6 words to talk about the weather.	65, 66, and 67
	☐ name at least 10 sports and kinds of exercise.	67 and 68
Conversation strategies	☐ ask follow-up questions to keep the conversation going.	70 and 71
	☐ react to things people say with *That's* . . . expressions.	71
Writing	☐ use imperatives to give instructions and advice.	73

Shopping

1 Do a crossword puzzle.

Vocabulary | **A** Complete the crossword puzzle. Write the names of the clothes.

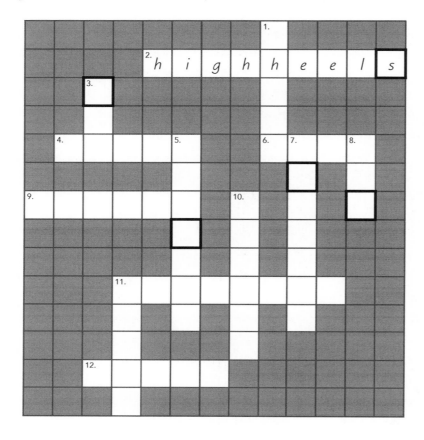

Down

1.   3.

5.   7.

8.  10.

11.

Across

2.  4.  6.

9.   11.  12.

B Now find the five highlighted letters in the puzzle. What do they spell?

___ ___ ___ ___ _s_

2 I want to spend some money!

Grammar | **Complete the conversations with the correct form of the verbs.**

1. **Mia**   Let's go shopping. I _need to buy_ (need / buy) some new clothes.

   Rick   OK. Where do you _____ (want / go) ?

   Mia   To the mall. I _____ (need / get)
   some new jeans. And I _____ (have / get)
   a couple of new suits for work.

   Rick   Listen. You go. I think I _____ (want / stay)
   home. I _____ (not need / buy) anything,
   and I _____ (want / check) my email.

   Mia   OK!

2. **Will**   I have a date with Megan tonight. She _____ (want / go)
   to an expensive restaurant.

   Ana   Really? Do you have any good clothes?
   Those old jeans are terrible. And you know Megan –
   she _____ (like / wear) designer clothes.

   Will   I know, but I _____ (like / wear) my jeans!
   And I _____ (not want / go) to a
   restaurant anyway. I _____ (want / go) to a movie.

   Ana   Oh, there's the phone. Hello? . . . Will, it's Megan. She's sick.

   Will   Oh, no! Well, now I _____ (not have / change) my clothes!

3 About you

Grammar and vocabulary | **Unscramble the questions. Then write true answers.**

1. A to the movies / do / like / What / to / wear / you ? _What do you like to wear to the movies?_
   B _____

2. A nice / have / When / do / to / clothes / you / wear ? _____
   B _____

3. A you / Do / a / have / uniform / to / wear ? _____
   B _____

4. A buy / Do / like / you / to / online / things ? _____
   B _____

5. A clothes / do / What / want / you / buy / to ? _____
   B _____

6. A do / go / like / Where / you / to / shopping ? _____
   B _____

1 Accessories

Vocabulary | Write the words under the pictures using *a* or *some*.

1. _some jeans_

2. _a dress_

3. _____

4. _____

5. _____

6. _____

7. _____

8. _____

9. _____

10. _____

11. _____

12. _____

13. _____

14. _____

15. _____

16. _____

2 Colors

Vocabulary | Complete the color words in the box. Then answer the questions, and complete the chart. Write three colors to answer each question, if possible.

r _e_ d   y_____w   b_____k   p_____e   w_____e
o_____e   b_____e   g_____n   b_____n   g_____y

What colors . . .			
do you like to wear?	*blue*		
are you wearing right now?			
do you never wear?			
are in your home?			
are your favorites?			
are popular right now?			
are in your country's flag?			

3 How much is this?

Grammar | **A** Complete the conversations. Use *this, that, these,*
or *those.*

1. Lena   Um, excuse me. How much is ___that___ dress?

    Clerk   The red dress? It's $325.

    Lena   Oh. And how about _____ shoes?

    Clerk   They're $149.

    Lena   Oh, really. And what about _____ T-shirts?
            Are they expensive, too?

    Clerk   They're $49.

    Lena   Oh, well. Thanks anyway.

2. Tito   Excuse me.

    Seller   Yes?

    Tito   How much are _____ umbrellas?

    Seller   They're $19.99.

    Tito $19.99? Really?

    Seller   Oh, wait. Sorry. _____ umbrella is $4.99.
             _____ umbrellas over here are $19.99.

    Tito   OK, so I want _____ umbrella, please.

B Look at the pictures. Write questions and answers.

1.
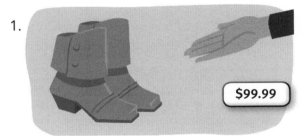
$99.99

A _How much are those boots?_
B _____

2.

$38

A _____
B _____

3.

$40

A _____
B _____

4.
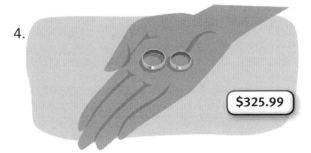
$325.99

A _____
B _____

Can I help you?

1 Um, uh, oh!

Complete the chart with the "conversation sounds" and expressions in the box.

| ✓ I know. | Let's see. | Really? | Uh, | Um, | Yeah. |
| Let me think. | Oh. | Right. | Uh-huh. | Well, | |

You want to show you agree.	You are surprised.	You need time to think.
I know.		

2 About you

Answer the questions with true information. Start each answer with a "time to think" expression.

1. What's your favorite color?

   Let me think. . . . I guess it's green.

   _____

2. What's your favorite thing to wear?

   _____

   _____

3. How often do you shop online?

   _____

   _____

4. How much do jeans cost these days?

   _____

   _____

5. How many birthday presents do you have to buy this month?

   _____

   _____

6. Does your family like to shop for clothes together?

   _____

   _____

3 Are you listening?

Conversation
strategies | **Complete the conversation with the correct expressions.**

Roberto   Mom, I have to get some things for college.

Mother   _____Uh-huh._____ What do you need to get?
          (Uh-huh. / Let me think.)

Roberto   _____ . . . I need to get a new computer and . . .
          (Um, let's see. / Really!)

Mother   _____ They're expensive.
          (Let me think. / Oh, really?)

Roberto   I know. But I have to go online a lot for my classes.

Mother   Well, OK. And what else do you want?

Roberto   _____ I want to get a new cell phone and . . .
          (Uh-huh. / Uh, well . . .)

Mother   _____ I'm surprised. I mean,
          (Oh, / Um,)

          you usually don't call, so . . .

Roberto   Well, I text sometimes. Anyway, _____ Oh, yes, and
                                        (let's see. / uh-huh.)

          I have to get some new sneakers.

Mother   _____ You really need new sneakers. Those sneakers are really old.
          (Let me think. / Uh-huh.)

Roberto   And what else? _____ What else do I need to get?
                         (Oh, really? / Uh, let's see.)

Mother   Well, there's one more thing you need to get . . .

Roberto   What's that?

Mother   A job! You need to pay for these things!

1 Online shopping

Reading **A** Read the article. Who likes to shop online? Who doesn't like to shop online? Check (✓) the correct boxes.

	Likes to shop online	**Doesn't like to shop online**
Sarah	☐	☐
Matt	☐	☐
Kevin	☐	☐
Susana	☐	☐

Do you like to shop online?

These days *everything* is for sale online – from movie tickets and food, to cars and houses. More and more people download music, movies, magazines, and books. It's easy and convenient. But not *everyone* likes to shop online.

Sarah Cho

"I never shop on the Internet because I like to pay cash. I don't have a credit card, and I don't want to get one. Also, I don't like to spend a lot of time online. I guess I'm not a big fan of shopping."

Matt Carson

"I work long hours – from 9:00 in the morning to 9:00 or 10:00 at night. A lot of stores close at 9:00. But the Internet never closes. I mean, I often shop at 1:00 in the morning. And the prices online are usually really cheap."

Kevin Parker

"There isn't a shopping center near my house. I have to drive an hour to the mall. Online shopping is very convenient. I buy movies, books, clothes, and food online. I never need to go out to a store."

Susana Rivera

"I like to shop with friends. We get up early and go to the mall together. We have a great time. We have lunch and look at the clothes together. When you shop online, you don't spend time with friends. You're alone."

B Read the article again. Then write *Sarah*, *Matt*, *Kevin*, or *Susana* next to the statements.

1. "I don't like to shop online or in stores!" _____*Sarah*_____

2. "I like to shop online because I never have to leave my home." _____

3. "I like to shop online because the prices aren't expensive." _____

4. "I don't like to shop online because I like to go to the mall with friends." _____

5. "I like to shop online because I don't have time during the day." _____

6. "I don't like to shop online because I don't like to go on the Internet." _____

2 What do you think?

Writing **A** Why do people like to shop online? Why do people hate to shop online? Check (✓) the correct box.

I like to shop online . . .	I hate to shop online . . .	Reasons
☐	☐	because I always buy things I don't need.
☐	☐	because it's easy to compare prices.
☐	☐	because it's convenient.
☐	☐	because you don't always have to pay sales tax.
☐	☐	because I often get "spam" emails from shopping websites.

B Answer these questions. Try to write more than *Yes* or *No*.

1. Do you live near a mall or shopping center? _____

2. Do you have time to shop during the week? _____

3. Do you like to go online? _____

4. Do you use a credit card? _____

C Write a short paragraph. Use your ideas from part B, and give reasons. Start like this:
I like to shop online because . . . **or** *I don't like to shop online because . . .*

_____

_____

_____

_____

Unit 8 Progress chart

What can you do? Mark the boxes. ✓ = I can . . . ? = I need to review how to . . .	To review, go back to these pages in the Student's Book.
Grammar ☐ use *like to*, *want to*, *need to*, and *have to* with other verbs. ☐ ask questions with *How much . . . ?* ☐ use *this*, *these*, *that*, and *those*.	76 and 77 78 and 79 79
Vocabulary ☐ name at least 12 kinds of clothes. ☐ name at least 12 accessories. ☐ name at least 8 color words.	75, 76, and 77 78 and 79 78
Conversation strategies ☐ use "time to think" expressions like *Um, . . .* and *Let's see . . . .* ☐ use *Uh-huh* and *Oh,* to show that I agree or I'm surprised.	80 81
Writing ☐ use *because* to give reasons.	83

A wide world

Lesson A / Sightseeing

 Take a tour!

Vocabulary **A Complete these suggestions for tourists.**

1. In South Korea, visit
   an island .

2. In New York, take pictures
   from a _____ .

3. In Germany, visit an old
   _____ .

4. See a _____ of a
   famous writer in Paris.

5. In Rio de Janeiro, spend a
   day at the _____.

6. In Egypt, walk around the
   _____ .

7. In London, see a famous
   _____.

8. Go up a _____ and
   get a good view of Tokyo.

9. Take a _____ of the
   city in Sydney.

Grammar and vocabulary **B Can you do any of the things in part A in your city or town? Write true sentences.**

1. _In my area, you can visit an island._ **or** _In my area, you can't visit an island._
2. _____
3. _____
4. _____
5. _____
6. _____
7. _____
8. _____
9. _____

2 What can you do in Toronto?

Grammar | **A** Read the guidebook. What can you do in Toronto? Complete the chart below.

TORONTO, CANADA

1. The CN Tower

Get a good view of the city from 553 meters (1,814 feet). A restaurant, shops, and a glass floor!

Hours: 10:00 a.m. to 11:00 p.m.

2. Casa Loma

Toronto's only castle. Call for a tour.

Open 9:30 a.m. to 5:00 p.m. (Last entry at 4:00 p.m.)

3. Yorkville

Walk around a lively historic neighborhood! Outdoor cafés, shops, and movie theaters.

4. The Art Gallery of Ontario

Hours: 10:00 a.m. to 5:30 p.m.

5. Centre Island

Take the ferry to Centre Island. Enjoy beautiful parks, great restaurants, and a children's amusement park.

Open all day.

6. Harbourfront Centre

Right on Lake Ontario, this huge center has everything for all the family. Ice skating, art, cafés, a music garden, shops, sailing, and boat tours. In the summer, there are outdoor concerts, a market, and special events.

Open from 10:00 a.m. to 9:00 p.m.

On a rainy day	On a sunny day	In the evening	With children
You can go to the Art Gallery of Ontario.			

B Complete the conversations with *can* or *can't*.

1.　Jill　What ___*can*___ you do at Harbourfront Centre?

　　Dan　Let's see . . . you _____ rent a boat. And at night, you _____ go to an outdoor concert.

　　Jill　Sounds great! _____ we go right now?

　　Dan　No, we _____ . It opens at 10:00 a.m., and it's only 7:30 a.m. now. It's really early.

　　Jill　Oh, you're right. Well, _____ we go to a café for breakfast?

　　Dan　Yes, we _____ do that. Let's go!

2.　Yoshi　I'm tired today. I don't want to go on another walking tour! Where _____ we go to relax?

　　Keiko　Let's go to Yorkville. We _____ have a nice lunch and see a movie.

　　Yoshi　OK, but we _____ spend a lot of money. We need to save our money for shopping!

1 What countries do you know?

Vocabulary   **A   Complete the names of the countries. Then write the countries in the chart below.**

1. S _p_ ai _n_
2. ____ ____ str ____ l ____ ____
3. ____ or ____ cc ____
4. C ____ st ____ ____ ic ____
5. R ____ ss ____ ____
6. M ____ x ____ c ____

7. P ____ r ____
8. Fr ____ nc ____
9. S ____ ____ th
   K ____ r ____ ____
10. Ch ____ n ____
11. Th ____ ____ l ____ nd

12. I ____ d ____ ____
13. J ____ p ____ n
14. C ____ n ____ d ____
15. Br ____ z ____ l

I know a lot about . . .			
I don't know a lot about . . .			
They speak English in . . .			
I love the food from . . .			
I don't want to go to . . .			

B   Look at the pictures. What kinds of food are these dishes? Write the nationalities.

1. _____Japanese_____

2. _____

3. _____

4. _____

C   Complete the chart.

Food I like	Food I don't like	Food I want to try	Food I can cook
Korean			French

2 **Where in the world?**

Vocabulary **Complete the crossword puzzle.**

1.									
2. A	N	3. T	A	R	C	T	4. I	C	5. A
		6.							
7.				8.					
	9.								
					10.				

Across

2. There are no cities in this cold, icy region.
6. This country is in both Europe and Asia.
7. This large region includes Japan and South Korea.
9. Beijing, Shanghai, and Hong Kong are in this country.
10. This long, thin country is in South America.

Down

1. They speak both French and English in this North American country.
3. They speak this language in Turkey.
4. Rome, Venice, and Milan are cities in this European country.
5. This large country is in Oceania.
8. They speak this language in Thailand.

3 **About you**

Grammar **Unscramble the questions. Then write true answers.**

1. can / sports / play / What / your best friend ?
   A *What sports can your best friend play?*
   B _____

2. food / mother / make / Can / Mexican / your ?
   A _____
   B _____

3. speak / you / languages / can / What ?
   A _____
   B _____

4. your / speak / English / parents / Can ?
   A _____
   B _____

1 What's this? What are these?

Conversation strategies | What are the things in the pictures? Write sentences. Use the words in the box.

| candy | dress | drink | ✓ musical instrument | sandwich | shoe |

1. *It's a kind of musical instrument.*
   It's called an erhu.

2. *They're a kind of*
   They're called

3. _____

4. _____

5. _____

6. _____

2 What's an *Inukshuk*?

Conversation strategies

Complete the sentences. Then unscramble the letters from the boxes to find the answer to the question.

1. A sneaker is a kind of $\boxed{s}$ _h_ _o_ _e_ .
2. A *tortilla* is kind of like a _p_ ___ ___ ___ $\boxed{a}$ ___ ___ .
3. A *balalaika* is like a _g_ ___ ___ $\boxed{t}$ ___ ___ .
4. *Gazpacho* is a kind of tomato ___ _s_ ___ $\boxed{}$ _p_ .
5. *Lassi* is kind of like a ___ ___ ___ _k_ _s_ ___ ___ $\boxed{e}$.
6. Volleyball is a kind of ___ _p_ ___ _r_ $\boxed{}$.

What's an *Inukshuk*?

It's like a _s_ ___ ___ _t_ ___ _e_ . You can see them in Alaska and Greenland.

3 It's a kind of pot.

Conversation strategies

Complete the conversations. Use *like*, *kind of like*, or *a kind of*.

1. A That's a beautiful dish!
   B Thanks. Actually, it's _a kind of_ pot. It's Japanese.
   A Can you cook with it? It looks so pretty.
   B Yeah! You can make Japanese food _____ *yosenabe* in it.
   A Like what?
   B Yosenabe. It's _____ soup.

2. A What can you buy at the market?
   B Well, you can buy food from different countries, things _____ fruit. You can buy durians . . .
   A What's a durian?
   B It's _____ fruit.
   A Really?
   B Yeah. It's _____ a melon.
   A Is it good?
   B Yes, I love it.

Exciting destinations

1 FAQs about Paris

Reading **A** Read the website. Write the correct question heading for each paragraph.

Where can you eat in Paris?	✓ What are great places to visit in Paris?
What do people wear in Paris?	How can I travel around Paris?

THE PARIS PAGE

Find out all you need to know about Paris! You can send your questions here for other travelers to answer. Or share your information about your trip to Paris.

Frequently Asked Questions (FAQs)

What are great places to visit in Paris?

You have to see the Eiffel Tower on your first visit. Then go to the Louvre. It's a very large and famous art museum. There are also beautiful gardens near it. After that, you can visit the Latin Quarter. It's a very old neighborhood. It has a lot of historic buildings, museums, and great shopping. **More**

It's easy to travel in Paris. There are trains, buses, and subways. Try the subway system, called the Metro. There are 301 Metro stations in the city. Every building in Paris is near a Metro station, so it's very convenient, too! **More**

Parisians love food. There are amazing cafés, bistros, and other kinds of restaurants everywhere in the city. You can relax at an outdoor café all day. Cafés open early in the morning and usually close late in the evening. **More**

Parisians like to "dress up" and wear designer clothes. They don't usually wear shorts, sneakers, or T-shirts to restaurants or concerts. You can wear casual clothes and shoes in Paris, but try to look nice. **More**

Next

B Read the website again. Then write *T* (true) or *F* (false) for each sentence. Correct the false sentences.

1. The Louvre is a famous garden in Paris. __F__ *The Louvre is a famous art museum in Paris.*

2. The Latin Quarter is a historic building. _____ _____

3. The Metro is a museum in Paris. _____ _____

4. A bistro is a kind of restaurant. _____ _____

5. Cafés open late in Paris. _____ _____

6. Parisians like to wear casual clothes when they go out. _____ _____

2 FAQs about your country

Writing | **A** Complete each sentence with three things about your city or country.
Make lists and use commas.

1. _El Salvador_ is famous for _its beautiful beaches, outdoor markets, and great food_ .

2. _____ is famous for _____ .

3. There are great places to see. You can visit _____ .

4. The people usually wear _____ .

B Imagine you are looking at a travel website about your country or city.
Write answers to these questions.

TRAVEL

1. I often travel there on business, but I don't usually have a lot of time. Where can I go and what can I see in one day?

   _____

   _____

   _____

2. I want to visit this summer, but I don't have a lot of money. What can I do for free?

   _____

   _____

   _____

3. Where can I meet local people? What traditional things can I see or do?

   _____

   _____

   _____

Unit 9 Progress chart

What can you do? Mark the boxes. ☑ = I can . . . ? = I need to review how to . . .	To review, go back to these pages in the Student's Book.
Grammar ☐ use *can* and *can't* to talk about things to do in a city.	86 and 87
☐ use *can* and *can't* to talk about ability.	88 and 89
Vocabulary ☐ use at least 10 new sightseeing words.	86 and 87
☐ name at least 15 countries and 5 regions.	88
☐ name at least 10 nationalities and 10 languages.	88 and 89
Conversation strategies ☐ use *a kind of* and *kind of like* to explain new words.	90
☐ use *like* to give examples.	91
Writing ☐ use commas to separate items in a list.	93

1 What did they do last night?

Grammar **What did these people do last night? What didn't they do? Complete two sentences for each picture. Use the simple past.**

stay home / visit her parents

1. Kate _stayed home_ .
   She _didn't visit her parents_ .

watch TV / practice her guitar

2. Rita _____ .
   She _____ .

study English / cook dinner

3. Mee-Sun _____ .
   She _____ .

play chess / watch a movie

4. Ali and Sam _____ .
   They _____ .

listen to music / email friends

5. Emil _____ .
   He _____ .

invite friends over / clean the house

6. Joe and Ken _____ .
   They _____ .

2 How was your weekend?

Grammar | Complete Grace's email. Use the simple past.

```
┌─────────────────────────────────────────────────────────────────────┐
│                          New Message                          ─ ▢ ✕   │
├─────────────────────────────────────────────────────────────────────┤
│      To: Paulina Lopez              ✉   📁   ☁   🗑                   │
│    From: Grace Chen                                                    │
│ Subject: How was your weekend?      🔍                                 │
├─────────────────────────────────────────────────────────────────────┤
```

Hi Paulina!

I really _enjoyed_ (enjoy) the weekend! I _____ (invite) a friend over on Saturday. She's my co-worker, and she's very nice. We _____ (play) tennis in the morning and _____ (stay) at the tennis club for lunch. Then we _____ (practice) yoga and _____ (walk) in the park.

In the evening, we _____ (watch) a movie and _____ (cook) a big dinner. We _____ (talk) a lot, but we _____ (not talk) about work. And we _____ (not watch) TV all day – a nice change!

Then on Sunday, I _____ (study) English and _____ (clean) the house. Hey! You _____ (not call) me on Sunday! Call me soon, OK? Tell me about your weekend.

Grace

3 About you

Grammar and vocabulary | Write true sentences about your weekend. Use the simple past. Add more information.

1. invite a friend over — _I invited a friend over for dinner._ **or** _I didn't invite a friend over for dinner._
2. stay home _____
3. study for an exam _____
4. clean the house _____
5. call a friend _____
6. check my email _____
7. chat online _____
8. practice my English _____
9. listen to music _____
10. rent a car _____
11. cook a big meal _____
12. exercise _____

1 A weekly planner

Grammar and vocabulary | Read Jenna's planner. Then complete the sentences below. Use the simple past of the verbs in the box.

SUNDAY	MONDAY	TUESDAY	WEDNESDAY
Movie with Meg 1:00 ✓	Read *The Pearl* ✓	Write book report on *The Pearl* ✓	Piano lesson 4:30 ✗
Romeo and Juliet – Grand Theater 2:00 ✗	Read art magazine ✗	Write history paper ✗	Doctor's appointment 2:00 ✓
Homework ✗	Homework ✓	Homework ✓	Homework ✓

THURSDAY	FRIDAY	SATURDAY
Call: Mom ✓ Felipe ✓ Lia ✓	Alison's party 7:30 ✓	Shopping! Need new: shoes ✗ jacket ✓
Make dinner 6:30 ✗	Mike 8:00 ✗	Homework ✗
Homework ✓	Homework ✓	

buy	do	go	have	make	read	✓see	write

1. On Sunday, Jenna ____saw____ a movie.
   She _didn't see_ a play.

2. On Monday, Jenna _____ a book in English.
   She _____ a magazine.

3. Jenna _____ a book report on Tuesday.
   She _____ a history paper.

4. Jenna _____ a doctor's appointment on Wednesday.
   She _____ a piano lesson this week.

5. On Thursday, Jenna _____ a lot of phone calls.
   She _____ dinner.

6. On Friday, Jenna _____ to a party.
   She _____ out with Mike.

7. Jenna _____ a new jacket on Saturday.
   She _____ new shoes.

8. Jenna _____ homework every school day.
   She _____ homework on the weekend.

About you

Grammar and vocabulary **A** Complete the questions in the questionnaire. Use the simple past of the verbs in the box. Then write true answers. Write more than *yes* or *no*.

| do | eat | ✓go | have | make | see | speak | take | write |

QUESTIONNAIRE: Did you . . . ?

1. ___Did___ you ___go___ out a lot last week?
Yes, I did. I went out every night last week. **or** _No, I didn't. I stayed home._

2. _____ you and your family _____ dinner in front of the TV last night?
_____

3. _____ you _____ anything interesting last weekend?
_____

4. _____ you _____ in a restaurant on Friday night?
_____

5. _____ your class _____ a test or an exam last week?
_____

6. _____ you _____ dinner every night last week?
_____

7. _____ your best friend _____ you an email yesterday?
_____

8. _____ your parents _____ a movie on Saturday night?
_____

9. _____ you _____ to a lot of friends in class yesterday?
_____

B Write a sentence about each day last week. Write one thing you did each day.

1. Monday _____
2. Tuesday _____
3. Wednesday _____
4. Thursday _____
5. Friday _____
6. Saturday _____
7. Sunday _____

1 Responding to news

A Complete the conversations. Circle and write the best response.

1. A I bought a new TV today.
   B _Good for you!_____

   (a.) Good for you!
   b. I'm sorry to hear that.
   c. Good luck!

2. A I'm 25 today!
   B _____

   a. I'm sorry to hear that.
   b. Good luck!
   c. Happy birthday!

3. A My wife had a baby girl last night.
   B _____

   a. Good for you!
   b. Happy birthday!
   c. Congratulations!

4. A I have a job interview today.
   B _____

   a. I'm sorry to hear that.
   b. Good luck!
   c. Happy birthday!

5. A I finally passed my English exam.
   B _____

   a. Thank goodness!
   b. I'm sorry to hear that.
   c. Good luck!

6. A I didn't get the job I wanted.
   B _____

   a. I'm sorry to hear that.
   b. Thank goodness!
   c. Good for you!

B Your friend tells you some news, and you respond. Write the conversations.

1. Your friend bought a new car, and he got a bargain.

   I bought a new car today. I got a bargain.   _Good for you!_

2. Your friend got 100% on her English exam.

3. Your friend finally got a job.

4. Your friend wanted to go on vacation, but he has no money.

2 You did?

A Complete the conversations with the expressions in the box.

✓You did?   You did?   You did?   Good luck!   I'm sorry to hear that.   Good for you.

---

1. Lilly Did you have a busy day?

   Beth Yeah, I'm exhausted. I went shopping downtown.

   Lilly ___*You*___ ___*did?*___ Did you buy anything?

   Beth Yes, I bought a new suit. And a blouse and shoes.

   Lilly _____ _____ _____

   Beth And then I had lunch with Maria, and we talked all

   afternoon. How about you?

   Lilly I cleaned the house, did the laundry, and made dinner.

   Beth _____ _____ That's great! I'm starving! Let's eat!

2. Jun Did you have a good week?

   José Actually, no. I had five exams.

   Jun _____ _____ That's awful. Did you pass?

   José Well, I passed three and failed two.

   Jun Oh. _____ _____ _____ _____ _____

   José And I have two exams tomorrow, too.

   Jun _____ _____ Study hard!

B Write two responses for each piece of news.

1. ⌈I had a terrible vacation in Hawaii.⌉

   ⌈ *You did?* *I'm sorry to hear that.* ⌉

2. ⌈I took my driver's test yesterday.⌉

   ⌈ _____ _____ ⌉

3. ⌈I wrote an article for a magazine last month.⌉

   ⌈ _____ _____ ⌉

4. ⌈My friend and I worked all weekend.⌉

   ⌈ _____ _____ ⌉

1 A busy birthday . . .

Reading **A** Look at the four pictures. Then read Peter's blog. Number the pictures in order from 1 to 4.

Friday, May 28 11:45 p.m.

I had a crazy day today. I had an English exam, and it's my birthday!

I had the exam at 8:30 this morning. I needed to study, so I woke up early – at 6:30 a.m. I took a shower, made some coffee, and studied for about an hour. Well, the coffee didn't work. I fell asleep!
I woke up at 8:20 with my head on my books. I had ten minutes before the test started!

I ran outside, got on my bike, and went to English class. I got there right at 8:30, but guess what! The teacher never came! My classmates and I waited about half an hour. Then we left. It's great. Now I can really study for the exam.

I had breakfast, and then I went to my next class – math. ☹ I think math is really hard, but I have to take it. My teacher talked for an hour. I wanted to write some notes, but I fell asleep. I need to borrow my friend's notes.

After I finished class, I met my friend Louisa, and we went to a movie together. It was my birthday, so she paid! Great! We saw a new romantic drama. You know, I usually like drama movies a lot, but I didn't like that movie very much.

When I got home from the movie, my mother called and sang "Happy Birthday" to me. Now I have to stay up and finish a paper for a class tomorrow. I hope I don't fall asleep again!

Posted by Peter Miller

0 comments

B Read the blog again. Then answer the questions. Give reasons for the answers.

1. Did Peter get up late? _No, he didn't. He needed to study._
2. Did Peter take an English exam? _____
3. Did he listen to his math teacher? _____
4. Did he go out with a friend? _____
5. Did Peter's mother call? _____
6. Do you think he's a good student? _____

2 My last birthday

Writing **A Read the blog on page 80 again. Match the two parts of each sentence.**

1. Peter studied when ___c___
2. Peter had breakfast after _____
3. When Peter went to his math class, _____
4. Peter finished classes. Then _____
5. Peter saw a movie before _____

a. he went home.
b. he fell asleep again.
✓c. he got up in the morning.
d. he met his friend Louisa.
e. he left his English class.

B Think about a day you remember well. Answer these questions. Write more than *yes* or *no*.

1. Did you work or have classes? _____
2. Did you go out with friends? _____
3. Did you do something fun? _____
4. Did you eat any of your favorite foods? _____
5. Did you go to any stores? _____
6. Did you get home late? _____

**C Write a paragraph for your own blog. Use your ideas from part B.
Use *before*, *after*, *when*, or *then*, if possible.**

I remember my last birthday. I _____

_____

_____

_____

_____

Unit 10 Progress chart

What can you do? Mark the boxes. ✓ = I can . . . ? = I need to review how to . . .	To review, go back to these pages in the Student's Book.
☐ make simple past statements with regular verbs.	98 and 99
☐ make simple past statements with irregular verbs.	100 and 101
☐ ask simple past *yes-no* questions.	101
☐ make simple past forms of at least 12 regular verbs.	98 and 99
☐ make simple past forms of at least 8 irregular verbs.	100 and 101
☐ use time expressions with the simple past.	101
☐ use responses like *Good for you!* and *Congratulations!*	102 and 103
☐ use *You did?* to show I'm listening, surprised, or interested.	103
☐ use *before*, *after*, *when*, and *then* to order events.	105

Grammar

Vocabulary

Conversation strategies

Writing

Looking back

Lesson A | My first . . .

1 Yesterday

Vocabulary | Complete the sentences. Use the words in the box.

| busy | ✓happy | nervous | nice | quiet | scared |

1. Yesterday was my birthday. My friends had a party for me, and I got a lot of presents. I was very ___happy___ .
2. My family and I live in a very small town. There are no clubs or movie theaters. My town is really _____ – especially at night.
3. I started a new job yesterday. I was really _____ of my new boss.
4. I had a lot of things to do yesterday. I was pretty _____ .
5. My best friend's parents are friendly. They're very _____ .
6. We had a French test last week. I was really _____ , but I passed.

2 It was fun!

Vocabulary | Choose the best two words to complete each sentence. Cross out the wrong word.

I remember my first driving lesson. Before I met the teacher, I was really ~~scary~~ / **nervous** / **scared**. But then I relaxed because he was very **nice** / **strict** / **friendly**. The lesson was **awful** / **good** / **fun** because I didn't make a lot of mistakes. I was pretty good. At the end of the lesson, I was **exhausted** / **lazy** / **tired**. It was hard work! After ten lessons, I took my test, but I didn't pass. I wasn't **awful** / **pleased** / **happy**. But I passed three weeks later. Now I can drive my dad's **nice** / **new** / **awful** car.

3 I remember . . .

Grammar | **Complete the conversations with *was, wasn't, were,* or *weren't*.**

1. **Sally**   Do you remember your first date, Grandpa?

   Grandpa   Yes. I ___was___ 16, and the girl _____ in my class.
   We _____ classmates. We went to the movies.

   Sally   _____ you nervous?

   Grandpa   No, I _____ . It _____ a lot of fun.

   Sally   Do you remember her name?

   Grandpa   Yes. Grandma!

2. **Paula**   I remember my first day of high school.
   It _____ a hot day, and I went with
   two of my friends.

   Kenton   _____ you scared?

   Paula   No, we _____ really scared, but I
   guess we _____ a little nervous.

   Kenton   _____ the teachers friendly?

   Paula   Yes, they _____ very nice.
   Thank goodness.

3. **Sun-Hee**   Do you remember your first college English class?

   Carla   Yes, it _____ last year. I _____ very good at
   English, and I made a lot of mistakes. My partner's
   English _____ very good, so he _____
   very happy with me!

   Sun-Hee   _____ he smart? I mean, intelligent?

   Carla   Yes, he _____ .

   Sun-Hee   So, was your first class fun?

   Carla   No, it _____ . In fact,
   it _____ awful.

1 About you

Grammar and vocabulary | **A Unscramble the questions. Then write true answers.**

1. trip or vacation / was / last / your / When ?

   A *When was your last trip or vacation?*

   B _____

2. go / did / Where / exactly / you ?

   A _____

   B _____

3. weather / like / was / the / What ?

   A _____

   B _____

4. you / there / do / did / What ?

   A _____

   B _____

5. were / there / How / you / long ?

   A _____

   B _____

Grammar | **B Read about Emi's first trip to the park with a friend. Write questions for the answers.**

"We weren't very old – I think I was eight, and my friend was ten. We went to the park, but my mother didn't know. We had a great time! We went swimming in the pool. I remember it was a beautiful day – warm and sunny. We were there about an hour. Then we got hungry, so we went home. When we got back, my mother wasn't too happy."

1. A *How old was Emi?*

   B Eight.

2. A _____

   B To the park.

3. A _____

   B Her friend.

4. A _____

   B They went swimming.

5. A _____

   B Warm and sunny.

6. A _____

   B About an hour.

2 *Get* and *go*

Vocabulary **A** **Which of these expressions do you use with *get*? Which do you use with *go*? Which can you use with *get* and *go*? Complete the chart.**

✓back	to bed	scared	swimming	to the movies	a view of something
✓lost	a gift	skiing	(an) autograph	snorkeling	along with someone
home	hiking	camping	on vacation	a bad sunburn	to see a concert / movie
sick	biking	married	up early or late	on a road trip	to the beach

get	*go*	*get* and *go*
lost		back

B **Complete the questions with *get* or *go*. Then write your own answers.**

1. A What time do you ___go **or** get___ to bed on weeknights?

    B _____

2. A How often do you _____ swimming?

    B _____

3. A Did you _____ a bad sunburn last year?

    B _____

4. A What did you _____ for your last birthday?

    B _____

5. A Can you think of someone you don't _____ along with?

    B _____

6. A Where do you want to _____ on vacation this year?

    B _____

7. A Do you _____ up early in the morning?

    B _____

Anyway, what did *you* do?

1 Asking questions

Conversation strategies | Complete each conversation with two questions.

1. **Sadie** How was your weekend?
   Bill It was awful. We went hang gliding. I hated it!
   Sadie That's too bad.
   Bill Yeah. Anyway, how about you?
   What did you do?
   Did you do anything special?
   Sadie Well, we rented a car and went camping.
   Bill That sounds nice.

2. **Dirk** Did you go out last night?
   Leo Yeah, I met a friend and went to a club.

   _____

   _____

   Dirk Oh, I went to the laundromat and did my laundry. I didn't do anything exciting.

3. **Shira** I went to the concert last Saturday.
   Jaz I did, too! The band sounded great.

   _____

   _____

   Shira Oh, it was fantastic. Well, anyway, it's 11:30.
   Jaz Yeah, it's late. See you tomorrow.

4. **Gabor** So, did you work last weekend?
   Koji Yeah, Saturday and Sunday. We were really busy.

   _____

   _____

   Gabor Let's see . . . I went shopping, um, and saw a movie. Then on Sunday, I played tennis, made dinner, . . .
   Koji I guess you were busy, too!

2 Well, anyway, . . .

A Use *anyway* three times in this conversation. Leave two of the blanks empty.

Mirka   Where were you last week? Were you away?

Arlen   Yes, I was in Mexico on business.

Mirka   Mexico? What was that like?

Arlen   Oh, great. The customers there are really nice. _____ I always enjoy my trips to Mexico. The people are so friendly.

Mirka   That's nice. _____ So you're traveling a lot these days.

Arlen   Yeah. About six times a year. _____ , what about you? Did you have a good week?

Mirka   Not bad. I had a lot of meetings – you know, the usual. _____ , do you want to go out tonight? We can have dinner maybe.

Arlen   Sure. We can meet after work.

Mirka   OK. Well, _____ , I have to go. See you later.

B Use the instructions to complete the conversations.

1. Friend   What do you usually do on the weekends?

   You   *I usually go out with friends. What about you?*
   (Answer. Then ask a question about your friend.)

   Friend   Me? I usually go to see a movie. Sometimes a friend and I go camping or hiking.

2. Friend   I'm enjoying my new job. My boss is OK, and the people are nice. We get along – it's a friendly place.

   You   That's nice. _____
   (Change the topic. Invite your friend for dinner tomorrow.)

   Friend   Tomorrow? Sounds great. What time? Seven?

3. Friend   What did you do for your last birthday?

   You   _____
   (Answer. Then end the conversation. It's late.)

   Friend   OK. Talk to you later.

4. Friend   So how was your weekend?

   You   _____
   (Answer. Then change the topic. Invite your friend to do something fun next weekend.)

   Friend   Sure. Sounds like fun.

A funny thing happened . . .

1 My first job

A Read the story. What are these people like? Match the names with the adjectives.

1. Diana ___a___
2. Joe _____
3. Megan _____
4. Rick _____

✓ a. friendly
 b. nervous
 c. good looking
 d. strict

Tell Us About Your First Job

Reader Megan Walker writes in with a story about her first job.

I remember my first job. I worked in an outdoor café one summer. It was called Sunny's. I got free drinks and food. My boss Diana was very friendly, and I got along well with her. Her husband Joe worked there, too, but he was really strict. On my first day, I was late because I got lost on the subway. After that, Joe was never too happy with me.

So, every day I served sandwiches and coffee. The café was really busy all the time. I wasn't a very good server, so I was often nervous. Also, I was always exhausted by the end of the day.

One day, I was really tired, so I asked to go home early. Joe looked angry, but he said, "OK. Fine." I left and went to the subway.

Then I met my friend Rick on the street. He was really good looking, and I liked him a lot. He said, "Do you want to go and eat something?" I said, "Yes. OK. Where?" And he said, "I know a café near here. Let's go there. They have good sandwiches."

So we went back to Sunny's and sat down to eat! We waited for about ten minutes before Joe finally came over to the table. He was very busy, so he didn't look at me. He said, "I'm sorry. One of the servers left early. Are you ready to order?" We stayed for an hour. I was lucky because my boss never saw me, but I had to pay for my sandwich and soda!

– Megan Walker
New York City

B Read Megan's story again. Then answer the questions.

1. Where did Megan work? *She worked at Sunny's.* _____

2. How did Megan get to work? _____

3. What kind of food did she serve? _____

4. What was the café like? _____

5. Why did she leave early one day? _____

6. Why did she go back to Sunny's? _____

7. How long did they stay at Sunny's? _____

2 He said, . . .

Writing **A** **Read the rest of the story. Rewrite their conversation after they leave the café. Use quoted speech. Add capital letters and correct punctuation (" " , . ?).**

Rick and I left the café and talked for a few minutes.

rick asked how did you like the café *Rick asked, "How did you like the café?"* _____

I said it's nice _____

he said the service wasn't very good _____

I said well one of the servers left early _____

rick said people are so lazy these days _____

I said yes I know _____

But I didn't tell Rick I was the server!

B **Think about a time you met a friend for the first time. Answer these questions.**

1. How old were you? _____

2. What was your friend's name? _____

3. How did you first meet? What happened? _____

4. What did you say when you first met? I said, "_____ ."

5. What did your friend say? She / He said, "_____ ."

C **Now write a story about meeting your friend. Use your ideas from part B.**

When we met, I was 13 and _____ . _____

_____

_____

Unit 11 Progress chart

What can you do? Mark the boxes. ☑ = I can . . . ? = I need to review how to . . .	To review, go back to these pages in the Student's Book.
Grammar ☐ make simple past statements and questions with *be*.	108 and 109
☐ ask simple past information questions.	110
Vocabulary ☐ name at least 12 words to describe people or experiences.	108 and 109
☐ name at least 4 new expressions with *go*.	111
☐ name at least 5 new expressions with *get*.	111
Conversation strategies ☐ ask and answer questions to show interest.	112
☐ use *Anyway* to change the topic or end a conversation.	113
Writing ☐ use capitals and punctuation in quoted speech.	115

1 Mmmmm!

Vocabulary | **Write the names of the foods. Then find the words in the puzzle. Look in these directions (→ ↓).**

1. _meat_

2. _seafood_

3. _____

4. _____

5. _____

6. _____

7. _____

8. _____

F	F	V	C	A	R	R	O	T	S
R	X	E	B	I	B	E	E	F	S
U	O	G	A	X	R	M	E	A	T
I	A	E	N	S	E	I	S	T	A
T	E	T	A	E	A	L	L	C	E
G	G	A	N	A	D	K	F	H	P
P	G	B	A	F	R	U	I	E	P
O	S	L	S	O	P	P	D	E	A
T	F	E	N	O	U	D	L	S	S
A	I	S	Z	D	I	H	G	E	T
T	S	H	R	I	C	E	F	Q	A
O	H	C	H	I	C	K	E	N	M
E	C	U	C	U	M	B	E	R	S
S	H	E	L	L	F	I	S	H	Z

9. _____

10. _____

11. _____

12. _____

14. _____

13. _____

15. _____

16. _____

17. _____

18. _____

2 An invitation to dinner

Grammar | **A** Read the invitation. Then circle the correct words to complete the emails.

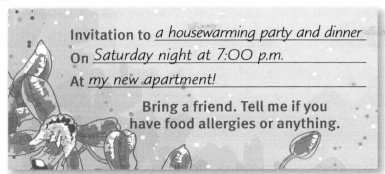

Invitation to *a housewarming party and dinner*
On *Saturday night at 7:00 p.m.*
At *my new apartment!*

Bring a friend. Tell me if you have food allergies or anything.

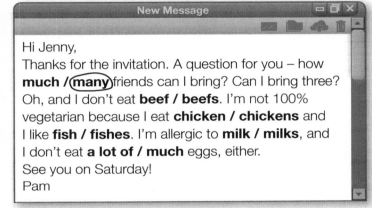

New Message

Hi Jenny,
Thanks for the invitation. A question for you – how
much / (many) friends can I bring? Can I bring three?
Oh, and I don't eat **beef / beefs**. I'm not 100%
vegetarian because I eat **chicken / chickens** and
I like **fish / fishes**. I'm allergic to **milk / milks**, and
I don't eat **a lot of / much** eggs, either.
See you on Saturday!
Pam

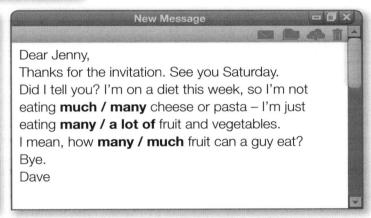

New Message

Dear Jenny,
Thanks for the invitation. See you Saturday.
Did I tell you? I'm on a diet this week, so I'm not
eating **much / many** cheese or pasta – I'm just
eating **many / a lot of** fruit and vegetables.
I mean, how **many / much** fruit can a guy eat?
Bye.
Dave

B Write your own email to Jenny. Tell her about these foods.

- food you like
- food you don't like
- food you eat a lot of
- food you don't eat a lot of

New Message

Dear Jenny,
Thanks for the invitation to the party. _____
_____
_____
_____
_____
_____

3 About you

Grammar and vocabulary | Complete the questions with *How much* or *How many*. Then write your own answers.

1. *How many* _____ students in your class are vegetarians? _____
2. _____ milk does your family buy every week? _____
3. _____ times a week do you eat chicken? _____
4. _____ shellfish do you eat? Do you eat a lot? _____
5. _____ of your friends are picky eaters? _____
6. _____ cans of soda do you drink a day? _____

What's for dinner?

1 At the supermarket

Vocabulary | **Write the words under the pictures. Then write the food in the chart below.**

1. _apples_

2. _____

3. _____

4. _____

5. _____

6. _____

7. _____

8. _____

9. _____

10. _____

11. _____

12. _____

13. _____

14. _____

15. _____

16. _____

17. _____

18. _____

19. _____

20. _____

meat and seafood	fruit	vegetables	other
	apples		

2 What would you like?

Grammar | **Complete the conversations. Use *would you like* or *'d like*.**

1. Jim   What _would you like_ ?
    Megan I _____ ice cream, please.
    Jim   _____ chocolate sprinkles?
    Megan Yes, please.

2. Server Good evening. _____ something to drink?
    Dan   Oh, just water, please.
    Server OK. And what _____ to eat?
    Dan   Um, I _____ the salmon, please.
    Server _____ some green beans with it?
    Dan   Actually, I _____ some spinach, please.

3. Greg   Where _____ to go for dinner?
    Sheila Oh, I don't know. I _____ to go
            somewhere around here.
    Greg   _____ to try the new Thai restaurant?
    Sheila Oh, yes! I _____ something spicy.

3 *Some* or *any*

Grammar | **Complete the conversations with *some* or *any*.**

1. Ming   Polly, try _some_ lamb.
    Polly Gosh, it's hot! I need _____ water . . . now!
    Ming   Here. Drink _____ soda.

2. John   Do you have _____ chocolate cookies?
    Ken   No, but we have _____ peanut butter cookies.
    John   OK, I'll take _____ .

3. Sara   Would you like _____ potato chips?
    Craig Yeah, but I don't have _____ money.
    Sara   Oh, and I don't have _____ , either.

1 Something for lunch

Conversation strategies | Complete the conversation with *or something* or *or anything*.

Trish Do you go out for lunch every day or . . . ?

Pete Well, I don't usually eat lunch. I don't like to eat a big meal *or anything* at lunchtime.

Trish No? You don't have a snack _____ ?

Pete Well, I sometimes have a hot drink, like hot chocolate _____ .

Trish Well, I'm hungry – I'd like a sandwich _____ . Would you like something to eat?

Pete Well, maybe . . .

Trish How about a salad _____ ?

Pete Yes, OK. Actually, I'd like a chicken sandwich. Oh, let's get some ice cream _____ , too. I guess I *am* hungry!

2 About you

Conversation strategies | Answer the questions. Write true answers. Use *or something* or *or anything*.

1. Are you a picky eater?   *Well, I don't eat fish or shrimp or anything.*

2. What do you usually have for dinner?   _____

3. How about lunch?   _____

4. What do you like to order in restaurants?   _____

5. What do you drink with meals?   _____

6. What kinds of snacks do you like?   _____

3 Would you like to go out or . . . ?

Complete the conversations. Which questions can end with or . . . ? Add or . . . where possible.

1. **Paul** What would you like for dinner tonight _____?
   Would you like to go out _or . . ._?

   Val Yes, please! I'd love to eat out.

   Paul That's great. So can I choose the restaurant _____?

   Val Sure.

   Paul Let's see . . . would you like a pizza _____?

   Val Um, I don't want Italian tonight. How about an Asian place? Do you like Korean or Thai _____?

   Paul Uh, I don't really care for spicy food.

   Val Let me think . . . do you want to get a hamburger _____?

   Paul Yeah! With maybe some French fries and some cookies.

   Val OK! Stop! I'm starving! Let's go!

2. **Kate** It's my birthday today.

   Sally Happy birthday! Do you have plans _____?

   Kate I had plans, but my friend just called. He's sick.

   Sally That's terrible! I know. Let's eat at my house. I can cook some steaks or something. What do you think _____?

   Kate That's very nice, thanks, but I'm a vegetarian.

   Sally Oh. Do you eat pasta _____?

   Kate Well, I can't eat pasta or anything heavy right now. I'm on a diet.

   Sally OK. No pasta. What would you like _____?

   Kate Do you have any fruit _____?

   Sally Sorry. I ate the last banana this morning before I went to work. I have some carrots. . . .

   Kate Let's stop at the supermarket on our way to your house.

1 Healthy fast food

Reading | **A Read the blog post. Find the answers to these questions.**

1. Where did the writer eat breakfast? _____

2. What breakfast food does the writer recommend? _____

3. How many calories were in the writer's lunch? _____

TASTES GOOD, AND GOOD FOR YOU!

We often think of fast food as hamburgers, fried chicken, hot dogs, and French fries. However, some fast-food restaurants are starting to offer healthy foods, too. But how healthy is "healthy" fast-food, and how does it taste? I went to some famous fast-food restaurants last week to find the answer and was pleasantly surprised. Here are the two healthy fast-food choices I recommend.

BURGER RESTAURANTS: OATMEAL, PLEASE!

Many burger restaurants open early and serve breakfast, too. One popular restaurant chain has a breakfast with more than 1,000 calories. That's about half the calories you need for a whole day! For a healthy option, you can now choose apple slices (15 calories), fruit and nuts (210 calories), or oatmeal (290 calories). I tried the oatmeal, and it was delicious!

MEXICAN RESTAURANTS: I'D LIKE IT IN A BOWL

I love Mexican fast food as a special treat, but I'm pleased to see that my favorite taco restaurant now has a lot of healthy choices on the menu. A taco salad with beef and cheese is about 600 calories. However, I went for chicken. You can make your own meal with chicken, rice, tomatoes, and other healthy foods. I tried it for lunch. I got it in a bowl and said no to the tortilla chips. It was very tasty and only 450 calories.

Do you know any great, healthy fast-food places? Tell us in the comments section.

B Read the blog post again. Then choose the correct words to complete these sentences.

1. The writer wanted to try some **hamburgers / healthy food** last week.

2. He thinks that 1,000 calories **is / is not** a lot for breakfast.

3. He **enjoyed / didn't enjoy** the oatmeal.

4. He had **taco salad / chicken** for lunch.

5. He **ate / didn't eat** tortilla chips with his lunch.

6. His lunch was **very / not very** healthy.

2 Restaurant reviews

Writing **A** Jill Heacock is a restaurant reviewer. She ate at the Seafood Palace last week, and she loved it. Circle the correct words to complete Jill's review.

THIS WEEK'S RESTAURANT: **THE SEAFOOD PALACE**   ★ ★ ★ ★

by Jill Heacock

Last week, I went to the Seafood Palace – it's a **terrible /** (**wonderful**) restaurant. I loved it. I was there on a busy night, and the atmosphere was **fun / formal**. The food was **awful / delicious**, and every dish came to the table **cold / hot**. I really liked the shrimp. Very tasty! The service was **excellent / slow**, the servers were really **friendly / lazy**, and the meal was **cheap / expensive**. I only spent $12!

The Seafood Palace is a good place to hang out with friends or have dinner with your family. Try it!

B Imagine you are a restaurant reviewer. You ate at a restaurant, and you hated it. Write your review.

THIS WEEK'S RESTAURANT: _____   ★

by _____

Last week, I went to _____ – it's a terrible restaurant! _____

_____

_____

_____

_____

_____

Unit 12 Progress chart

What can you do? Mark the boxes. ✓ = I can . . . ? = I need to review how to . . .	To review, go back to these pages in the Student's Book.
☐ use countable and uncountable nouns.	118 and 119
☐ make statements and questions with *much, many,* and *a lot of.*	118 and 119
☐ make statements and questions with *some, any,* and *not any.*	120 and 121
☐ make offers and requests with *would like.*	121
☐ name at least 5 categories of food.	118 and 119
☐ name at least 25 different foods.	118, 119, and 120
☐ use *or something* and *or anything.*	122
☐ use *or . . . ?* in *yes-no* questions to make them less direct.	123
☐ use expressions to talk about restaurants.	124 and 125

Grammar

Vocabulary

Conversation strategies

Writing

Illustration credits

Ken Batelman: 42   **Harry Briggs:** 15, 61 *(4 at bottom)*, 69   **Domninic Bugatto:** 8, 23, 27, 38, 59, 78   **Cambridge University Press:** 67
Matt Collins: 22, 54   **Chuck Gonzales:** 5, 11, 26, 45, 80   **Cheryl Hoffman:** 3, 24, 47, 61 *(2 at top)*   **Jon Keegan:** 19, 51, 94, 95
Frank Montagna: 2, 13, 21, 53, 82, 83   **Greg White:** 7, 16, 37, 79   **Terry Wong:** 30, 46, 63, 74, 86   **Filip Yip:** 70

Photo credits

Text credits

While every effort has been made, it has not always been possible to identify the sources of all the material used, or to trace all copyright holders. If any omissions are brought to our notice, we will be happy to include the appropriate acknowledgements on reprinting.

Special thanks to Kerry S. Vrabel for his editorial contributions.

The top 500 spoken words

This is a list of the top 500 words in spoken North American English. It is based on a sample of four and a half million words of conversation from the Cambridge International Corpus. The most frequent word, *I*, is at the top of the list.

1. I	40. really	79. see
2. and	41. with	80. how
3. the	42. he	81. they're
4. you	43. one	82. kind
5. uh	44. are	83. here
6. to	45. this	84. from
7. a	46. there	85. did
8. that	47. I'm	86. something
9. it	48. all	87. too
10. of	49. if	88. more
11. yeah	50. no	89. very
12. know	51. get	90. want
13. in	52. about	91. little
14. like	53. at	92. been
15. they	54. out	93. things
16. have	55. had	94. an
17. so	56. then	95. you're
18. was	57. because	96. said
19. but	58. go	97. there's
20. is	59. up	98. I've
21. it's	60. she	99. much
22. we	61. when	100. where
23. huh	62. them	101. two
24. just	63. can	102. thing
25. oh	64. would	103. her
26. do	65. as	104. didn't
27. don't	66. me	105. other
28. that's	67. mean	106. say
29. well	68. some	107. back
30. for	69. good	108. could
31. what	70. got	109. their
32. on	71. OK	110. our
33. think	72. people	111. guess
34. right	73. now	112. yes
35. not	74. going	113. way
36. um	75. were	114. has
37. or	76. lot	115. down
38. my	77. your	116. we're
39. be	78. time	117. any

The top 500 spoken words

118. he's	161. five	204. sort
119. work	162. always	205. great
120. take	163. school	206. bad
121. even	164. look	207. we've
122. those	165. still	208. another
123. over	166. around	209. car
124. probably	167. anything	210. true
125. him	168. kids	211. whole
126. who	169. first	212. whatever
127. put	170. does	213. twenty
128. years	171. need	214. after
129. sure	172. us	215. ever
130. can't	173. should	216. find
131. pretty	174. talking	217. care
132. gonna	175. last	218. better
133. stuff	176. thought	219. hard
134. come	177. doesn't	220. haven't
135. these	178. different	221. trying
136. by	179. money	222. give
137. into	180. long	223. I'd
138. went	181. used	224. problem
139. make	182. getting	225. else
140. than	183. same	226. remember
141. year	184. four	227. might
142. three	185. every	228. again
143. which	186. new	229. pay
144. home	187. everything	230. try
145. will	188. many	231. place
146. nice	189. before	232. part
147. never	190. though	233. let
148. only	191. most	234. keep
149. his	192. tell	235. children
150. doing	193. being	236. anyway
151. cause	194. bit	237. came
152. off	195. house	238. six
153. I'll	196. also	239. family
154. maybe	197. use	240. wasn't
155. real	198. through	241. talk
156. why	199. feel	242. made
157. big	200. course	243. hundred
158. actually	201. what's	244. night
159. she's	202. old	245. call
160. day	203. done	246. saying

The top 500 spoken words

247. dollars	290. started	333. believe
248. live	291. job	334. thinking
249. away	292. says	335. funny
250. either	293. play	336. state
251. read	294. usually	337. until
252. having	295. wow	338. husband
253. far	296. exactly	339. idea
254. watch	297. took	340. name
255. week	298. few	341. seven
256. mhm	299. child	342. together
257. quite	300. thirty	343. each
258. enough	301. buy	344. hear
259. next	302. person	345. help
260. couple	303. working	346. nothing
261. own	304. half	347. parents
262. wouldn't	305. looking	348. room
263. ten	306. someone	349. today
264. interesting	307. coming	350. makes
265. am	308. eight	351. stay
266. sometimes	309. love	352. mom
267. bye	310. everybody	353. sounds
268. seems	311. able	354. change
269. heard	312. we'll	355. understand
270. goes	313. life	356. such
271. called	314. may	357. gone
272. point	315. both	358. system
273. ago	316. type	359. comes
274. while	317. end	360. thank
275. fact	318. least	361. show
276. once	319. told	362. thousand
277. seen	320. saw	363. left
278. wanted	321. college	364. friends
279. isn't	322. ones	365. class
280. start	323. almost	366. already
281. high	324. since	367. eat
282. somebody	325. days	368. small
283. let's	326. couldn't	369. boy
284. times	327. gets	370. paper
285. guy	328. guys	371. world
286. area	329. god	372. best
287. fun	330. country	373. water
288. they've	331. wait	374. myself
289. you've	332. yet	375. run

The top 500 spoken words

376. they'll
377. won't
378. movie
379. cool
380. news
381. number
382. man
383. basically
384. nine
385. enjoy
386. bought
387. whether
388. especially
389. taking
390. sit
391. book
392. fifty
393. months
394. women
395. month
396. found
397. side
398. food
399. looks
400. summer
401. hmm
402. fine
403. hey
404. student
405. agree
406. mother
407. problems
408. city
409. second
410. definitely
411. spend
412. happened
413. hours
414. war
415. matter
416. supposed
417. worked

418. company
419. friend
420. set
421. minutes
422. morning
423. between
424. music
425. close
426. leave
427. wife
428. knew
429. pick
430. important
431. ask
432. hour
433. deal
434. mine
435. reason
436. credit
437. dog
438. group
439. turn
440. making
441. American
442. weeks
443. certain
444. less
445. must
446. dad
447. during
448. lived
449. forty
450. air
451. government
452. eighty
453. wonderful
454. seem
455. wrong
456. young
457. places
458. girl
459. happen

460. sorry
461. living
462. drive
463. outside
464. bring
465. easy
466. stop
467. percent
468. hand
469. gosh
470. top
471. cut
472. computer
473. tried
474. gotten
475. mind
476. business
477. anybody
478. takes
479. aren't
480. question
481. rather
482. twelve
483. phone
484. program
485. without
486. moved
487. gave
488. yep
489. case
490. looked
491. certainly
492. talked
493. beautiful
494. card
495. walk
496. married
497. anymore
498. you'll
499. middle
500. tax